TEA

FIT FOR A

QUEEN

TEA
FIT FOR A
QUEEN

◆ RECIPES & DRINKS FOR AFTERNOON TEA ◆

In association with
HISTORIC ROYAL PALACES

EBURY
PRESS

5 7 9 10 8 6

Published in 2014 by Ebury Press, an imprint of Ebury Publishing

A Random House Group Company

Text © Historic Royal Palaces 2014
Layout and design © Ebury Press 2014

Picture credits:
All food photography by Jan Baldwin
All other photography by Historic Royal Palaces (pages 6, 7, 8, 18, 32, 82, 83)

The turquoise and gold fine bone china 'Royal Palace' tea set featured in many
of the photographs is exclusive to Historic Royal Palaces, and is avaliable from
their online shop at www.hrp.org.uk

A CIP catalogue record for this book is available from the British Library
The Random House Group Limited supports the Forest Stewardship Council®
(FSC®), the leading international forest-certification organisation. Our books
carrying the FSC label are printed on FSC®-certified paper. FSC is the only
forest-certification scheme supported by the leading environmental
organisations, including Greenpeace. Our paper procurement policy
can be found at www.randomhouse.co.uk/environment.

MIX
Paper from
responsible sources
FSC® C015829

To buy books by your favourite authors and register for offers visit
www.randomhouse.co.uk

Writer and project editor: Imogen Fortes
Recipes and food stylist: Emma Marsden
Design and art direction: Turnbull Grey
Photographer: Jan Baldwin
Prop stylist: Tabitha Hawkins
Proofreader: Laura Nickoll

Printed and bound in Italy by Printer Trento S.r.l.
ISBN 9780 09195 871 8

CONTENTS

INTRODUCTION
BY LUCY WORSLEY
CHIEF CURATOR OF
HISTORIC ROYAL
PALACES

When I'm happy, I celebrate with a cup of tea. When I'm sad, I console myself with a cup of tea. As a living cliché of a British person, tea is central to my life. But talk to the health-conscious and they'll warn you that the caffeine in tea is addictive, and dangerous.

The Georgians would have agreed! In the eighteenth century, the still-novel drink of tea was feared as an intoxicant. Tea is a 'detestable, fatal liquor', writes the Earl of Bristol in 1731. Drinking it will bring you 'near to death's door' and will 'demonstrably hasten your passage through it many years before you need otherwise experience it'.

The drink made by stewing the leaves of the Chinese tea plant in water only became fashionable in these islands after a famous case of sea-sickness. People in London began to hear about this new Chinese drink in the years of the Restoration, when King Charles II returned to his throne after Oliver Cromwell's Commonwealth.

Everyone's favourite seventeenth-century diarist, Samuel Pepys, first tasted tea in 1660. He described having 'a cup of tee (a China drink) of which I never had drank before' on 25th September. (Elsewhere in his diary Pepys, keen for novelty, describes his first sip of the other new drinks of orange juice, and hot chocolate, which he tries as a cure for a hangover.)

But it took the arrival of Charles II's new young royal bride in 1662 to make tea catch on as our national drink. Catherine of Braganza had endured a terrible ocean voyage to reach England from her home in the south. Her native Portugal had good trading links with the East, and tea was popular there.

Upon landing in Britain, Catherine was still feeling queasy, and asked for a cup of tea. Blank faces greeted her among the British, and the ale she was offered as an alternative didn't quite fit the bill. So the Portuguese princess popularised tea among the members of her court, and of course, they all became addicted.

Tea-drinking was at first an expensive habit, as the leaves had to be imported such a great distance. The holds of the tea clippers bringing tea from the East were also packed with another necessary part of a tea party: delicate china tea dishes (as teacups were known, before they had handles). These were originally incidental to the business of importing tea: the heavy chests of porcelain provided useful ballast for the ships. But then they became highly desirable in their own right.

Tea dishes of the seventeenth century, imported from the East, rarely matched, and the idea that cups should form an identical set did not develop until home-grown British ceramic production took off in the eighteenth century. If you were a rich Stuart or Georgian lady, you would store your tea leaves in a locked caddy, so that your servants couldn't pinch them, and you would host tea parties in the afternoon for your lady friends.

These were occasions to show off your drawing room, your china and your best dress too. Tea, a sociable drink best enjoyed with friends, forms something of an unlikely alliance with feminism. Until tea came along, the standard social gathering tended to be men drinking ale. The new all-female tea parties took place not in the evening but in the afternoon, when the men were busy, and one amusing Georgian print shows husbands, excluded, creeping up to the window to see what their wives were saying about them.

Because tea was so expensive, it did have connotations of luxury and danger. At first only the aristocracy could afford to use it to cure the cares of a lover lost or a gambling debt gamed. (A wise Georgian matron would advise 'now leave complaining, and bring your Tea'.)

By the late eighteenth century, though, tea-drinking was filtering down through society, and so too teapots and teacups were to be found in ordinary people's houses. In late-Georgian Britain, even servants could insist on an allowance of tea as part of the conditions of their employment.

Tea had become so central to people's lives that in 1773 it became the focus for the American colonists' complaints against the British government. 'No taxation without representation' in Parliament, they insisted, and in the 'Boston tea party', chests of tea were thrown into Boston harbour after the Americans refused to pay tax on it.

This pretty little book tells you everything you need to know to throw a spectacular tea party. As well as being the drink of queens, tea is even fit for a royal wedding.

After the famous double royal marriage of 1818, when at the Historic Royal Palace of Kew no less than two princes married two princesses in the same room on the same day, Queen Charlotte refreshed the whole party with... a cup of tea!

CAKES, PASTRIES AND TARTS

ROSE AND ALMOND CAKE

This delightfully light, fragrant cake is made with ground almonds,
scented with rose and decorated with sugar-crusted rose petals – perfect
for a summery afternoon tea. Make sure you buy unsprayed rose petals
and be as lavish as you like with the decoration.

Serves 12

125g plain flour, plus extra
for dusting

6 large eggs

175g caster sugar, plus
extra for the rose petals

50g ground almonds

1 tsp rose water

40g unsalted butter,
melted and cooled

a little vegetable oil, for
greasing

For the icing and
decoration

1 egg white

fresh, unsprayed rose
petals

100g icing sugar

½ tbsp rose water

edible pink food colouring

Preheat the oven to 180°C/gas 4. Brush the inside
and rim of a 24cm round ring tin with vegetable oil.
Dust with flour, then shake out any excess.

Whisk the eggs and sugar together in a large bowl
until the mixture is thick and moussey and has doubled
in volume. Sift over the flour and ground almonds then
carefully pour the rose water and melted butter around
the edge. Fold everything together gently using a large
metal spoon, making sure that all the flour has been
incorporated.

Spoon into the prepared tin and bake in the oven
for 25–30 minutes until the top springs back lightly
when pressed.

Allow the cake to cool in the tin for 5 minutes, then
gently ease the edge of it away from the tin. Turn
out on to a wire rack and allow to cool completely.

Lightly beat the egg white in a small bowl until frothy
then use to brush over each rose petal. Dust with
caster sugar.

For the icing, mix together the icing sugar, rose water
and around 2 teaspoons of water. Stir until smooth.
Add a drop of pink food colouring and stir until it's the
shade you desire. Drizzle over the cake. Decorate with
the rose petals and allow to set before serving in slices.

CARROT CAKES WITH BUTTERCREAM

These dainty little cupcakes are small enough not to be considered extravagant yet bursting with luxuries. They can be decorated with a little marzipan carrot for a touch of fun or served gracefully iced as would befit a royal table.

Makes 12

125g light muscovado sugar

2 large eggs

75ml sunflower oil

200g self-raising flour

1 tsp ground cinnamon

1 tsp ground mixed spice

150g carrots, grated

100g sultanas

25g desiccated coconut

grated zest of 1 orange

For the buttercream and decoration

around 100g white marzipan

edible orange and green food colouring

40g unsalted butter, softened

75g icing sugar

150g cream cheese

Although carrot cake is a bake that abounds in riches, it was originally associated with frugality and resourcefulness. Canny bakers as far back as the Middle Ages have been using the natural sweetness of the humble carrot to substitute the far more costly sugar.

Preheat the oven to 180°C/gas 4. Line a 12-hole muffin tray with paper cases.

Whisk together the sugar, eggs and oil in a large bowl until mixed well. Sift over the flour and spices, then add the carrot, sultanas, coconut and orange zest and fold everything together. Spoon evenly into the muffin cases then bake in the oven for around 30 minutes until golden and a skewer inserted into the centre comes out clean. Transfer the cakes to a wire rack to cool.

To make the marzipan carrots, pull off 40g marzipan and set aside. Dip a cocktail stick into the orange colour then wipe it on to the remaining marzipan. Knead on a board until the marzipan is your desired colour. Knead the reserved piece with green. Divide the orange piece into 12 then roll each into the shape of a carrot, around 3cm long – teasing out a point at one end and squaring off the other end. Divide the green marzipan into 12 then roll each piece into a thin sausage. Divide into three – these are your stalks. Push a cocktail stick into the thick end of the carrot three times and push three green stalks into each hole. With a small sharp knife, mark horizontal lines down the length of each carrot, then set aside to dry out.

For the icing, beat the butter and icing sugar until soft and creamy then fold in the cream cheese. Ice each cake then push a carrot on top.

HAMPTON COURT PALACE

Meander along the banks of the River Thames
and you will happen upon the waterfront palace
of Hampton Court. An elegant red-brick Tudor frontage
masks its secret – Hampton Court is in fact two palaces,
each the work of a different monarch, reflecting their
respective eras and different architectural styles, though
equally imposing in their grandeur and elegance.

While Hampton Court is often most closely associated with Henry VIII, it was the monarch's closest political adviser, Cardinal Wolsey, who acquired the medieval manor in 1514, transforming it from a grand private house into a palace fit for a bishop with close ties to his king. The rich tapestries that still adorn many of the rooms are characteristic of Wolsey's era – sumptuous creations woven with gold and silver threads. By 1525 it was truly a palace, Wolsey had been promoted to Cardinal, and he formally presented it to Henry VIII, although he continued to add to the building. However, when poor Wolsey failed to secure the King a divorce from Katherine of Aragon, the Cardinal was out of favour, and in 1529 Henry removed him from Hampton Court forever.

Although Henry VIII moved between around 60 homes, Hampton Court was one of his grandest and most sumptuously decorated – his pleasure palace, where he feasted, hunted and enjoyed its countless recreational attractions. Over the course of his reign, Henry rebuilt his rooms there several times; with each new wife came ever more lavish lodgings; and both the Great Hall – his vast communal dining room – and kitchens (see pages 28–9) are magnificent examples of the scale of his extravagance and ostentation.

Henry's high-living gave way to a quieter period at the palace: his three children enjoyed Hampton Court as a country retreat from their claustrophobic London residences. But James I (1603–25), the first of the Stuart monarchs and a somewhat wayward royal, reprised Henry's mantle and Hampton Court was once again to become a party palace. His was an era of entertainment and intoxicating revelry. The Great Hall was transformed into a theatre where William Shakespeare and his troupe performed, and the palace hosted spectacular banquets and grand masques.

If walls could talk, the royal bedchamber would certainly have a few stories to tell. Secrecy, politics and scandal abounded at Hampton Court. In 1714 George I arrived from Hanover minus a queen (he divorced, then locked her up for adultery) but instead accompanied by what appeared to be two mistresses, known unkindly as 'The Elephant' and 'The Maypole'. Vicious rumours circulated about the pair, but in fact, Sophia von Kielmansegg (the fat one) was actually his half-sister and constant companion. His actual mistress, Melusine von Schulenberg (the tall one) was no beauty either, but was described as 'being duller than the king... consequently did not find him so'. More beautiful, and far from dull, was George II's principal mistress, Henrietta Howard, Queen Caroline's lady in waiting, who suffered the boorish George for over 20 years, one of the longest affairs in royal history.

When William III and Mary II acceded to the throne in 1689, Hampton Court acquired the second of its buildings – an elegant baroque edifice with scarlet brickwork, opulent painted interiors and formal gardens. The expansive gardens laid out for the King and Queen are exemplary of a grand era of gardening, and William's 'Wilderness Garden', his world-famous maze with its clipped hedges and vast network of pathways, remains a charming way to while away an afternoon at the palace.

Hampton Court had been a setting for marriages, births, family rivalries, and revelry, but in the 1730s it finally ceased to be a royal residence and became a retirement home for well-to-do ladies (mostly widows). Some of its colourful residents included Lady Baden-Powell, widow of the founder of the Boy Scouts, prominent suffragettes and Russian royal refugees. Finally, in 1838, the young Queen Victoria opened the palace to her subjects and today Hampton Court remains one of England's most intriguing historical tourist attractions and a proud expression of British stately architecture.

APPLE AND SPICE CAKE

A fruit-filled majestic cake, decorated with slices of apple and liberally coated in apricot jam. Using wholemeal flour and ground almonds not only complements the spices, it produces a wonderful firm texture making this a hearty, rustic autumnal treat.

Serves 16

2 Bramley or cooking apples (around 450g)

200g unsalted butter, softened, plus extra to grease

150g soft light brown sugar

3 medium eggs, at room temperature

175g self-raising wholemeal flour

75g ground almonds

grated zest of ½ lemon

1 tsp ground mixed spice

½ tsp ground ginger

a good pinch of ground cloves

a good pinch of ground cinnamon

splash of milk

2 tbsp apricot conserve

Preheat the oven to 190°C/gas 5. Grease and line a 20cm round, loose-bottomed, deep cake tin with greaseproof paper.

Peel and chop one of the apples and set aside.

Cream the butter and sugar together in a large bowl. Gradually beat in the eggs, a little at a time, then fold in the wholemeal flour, ground almonds, lemon zest, all the spices, chopped apple and a splash of milk.

Spoon into the prepared tin. Core the remaining apple and slice thinly. Arrange over the top of the cake. Bake in the oven for 1 hour until golden.

Cool in the tin for 5 minutes, then remove and transfer to a wire rack.

Sieve the apricot conserve to remove any lumps then brush all over the cake while it's still warm. Serve warm or cold.

VICTORIA SANDWICH

Queen Victoria had a very sweet tooth and Buckingham Palace kitchens worked feverishly to meet her requests for pastries. It seems fitting that the most beloved of British bakes should be named after the cake-loving monarch. Whether you remain true to the monarch's humble jam filling or opt for the decadent cream is well is up to you.

Serves 8–10

225g unsalted butter, softened, plus extra to grease

225g golden caster sugar

4 medium eggs, at room temperature

225g self-raising flour

To serve

strawberry jam

150ml double cream, whipped (optional)

icing sugar, to dust

Preheat the oven to 180°C/gas 4. Grease and line two 18cm round loose-bottomed cake tins with greaseproof paper.

Put the butter and sugar in a large bowl. Cream the two ingredients together using an electric hand whisk or a wooden spoon until the mixture is pale and creamy.

Whisk the eggs in a jug and gradually add them, a little at a time, to the butter mixture, whisking well between each addition. Stir in a spoonful of flour if the mixture looks as if it might curdle. Fold in the flour, along with 2 tablespoons of boiling water, which helps to lighten the finished cake.

Spoon evenly between the two prepared cake tins and bake in the oven for 20–25 minutes, until golden on top and firm to the touch. Turn out on to a wire rack and leave to cool completely.

Peel off any paper and place one cake on a serving plate. Spread with jam, then if you're opting for cream too, spoon it carefully on top. Sandwich with the other cake and dust with a little icing sugar to serve.

There is some question over the precise ingredients and method of presenting a Victoria sandwich. Certainly Queen Victoria would not have been able to sandwich her sponge with whipped cream as is often the case today, but the monarch would indeed have enjoyed the traditional jam in the middle and perhaps a dusting of sugar over the top.

DUNDEE CAKE

If legend is to be believed, Dundee cake was first baked in the sixteenth century for Mary Queen of Scots. Mary loved fruit cakes but didn't favour cherries, so a version made with almonds was created for the monarch instead.

Serves 8

125g unsalted butter, softened

125g golden caster sugar

3 medium eggs, at room temperature

125g self-raising flour

1 tsp ground mixed spice

75g sultanas

75g currants

1 heaped tbsp marmalade

75g ground almonds

whole blanched almonds, to decorate

Preheat the oven to 170°C/gas 3. Line a deep 16cm round cake tin with greaseproof paper.

Beat together the butter and sugar in a bowl until soft and creamy. Gradually beat in the eggs, a little at a time, then fold in the flour, spice, dried fruit, marmalade and ground almonds to make a smooth batter.

Spoon into the tin and arrange the almonds in circles around the edge and into the middle. Bake in the oven for 1–1¼ hours or until a skewer inserted into the centre comes out clean. Remove from the oven and transfer to a wire rack to cool.

Mary's wishes hold fast today for a true Dundee cake is immediately distinguishable from other types of fruit cake by its iconic appearance: the top is decorated with a pattern of whole blanched almonds.

HONEY MEAD CAKES

Mead – an alcoholic drink made from fermented honey and water – was made by monks in the Middle Ages. When Henry VIII dissolved the monasteries, production fell rapidly. These delicious, satisfying little cakes are firm favourites among visitors to the palaces.

Makes 12

25g currants or raisins

75ml mead

100g golden caster sugar

25g cloudy honey

125g unsalted butter, softened

grated zest of 1 orange

125g self-raising flour

25g wholemeal flour

For the orange icing and decoration

100g golden icing sugar

2–3 tbsp orange juice

1 orange

Preheat the oven to 180°C/gas 4. Line a 12-hole bun tin with cake cases.

Put the currants in a pan with the mead. Bring to the boil and simmer for 2–3 minutes then turn off the heat and set aside.

Whisk the sugar, honey and butter together in a bowl until light and fluffy. Beat in the orange zest then add the soaked currants and any leftover liquid and sift over the flours. Fold everything together with a large metal spoon.

Divide the mixture evenly among the cases and bake in the oven for 20–25 minutes. Transfer to a wire rack to cool.

For the icing, put the icing sugar in a bowl and gradually add the orange juice, stirring together until you've made a paste that's not too runny. Drizzle over each cake. Make curls of zest from the orange then put a good pinch of them on top of each round of icing. Allow to set before serving.

HENRY VIII'S KITCHENS

Henry VIII was a monarch renowned for his love of lavish abundance – whether it was women, food, palaces or sport, Henry indulged his passions on a grand scale. So when he took over Hampton Court Palace in 1529, one of the first projects he embarked upon was to increase the size of the palace kitchens.

While Henry's own meals were served to him in his lodgings from a private kitchen, he travelled with a vast entourage of around 600 courtiers, all of whom were entitled to meals at the palace twice a day and he needed kitchens large enough to provide for them.

By the time the builders had finished, Hampton Court boasted around 55 rooms devoted to food production, staffed by 200 people. Henry was a generous patron and the meals served were by no means meagre or uninspired. A Tudor diner at court, depending on their status, could expect to be served a wide range of fresh produce, from copious quantities of meat – roast beef or mutton and hearty stews – to freshly baked breads and a variety of fruit and vegetables grown in the palace gardens.

On feast days or special occasions, Henry would dine with the court, seated at a top table surrounded by his most favoured guests. Elaborate banquets, often lasting several hours, would be prepared, and included an array of luxury ingredients, including swan, venison, salmon and porpoise.

Henry is famous for having a sweet tooth and 'sweetmeats' crystallised or honeyed fruits, sugared almonds, jellies or marzipan sculptures) were an important part of his regal feast, all prepared in his confectionery kitchens. During the sixteenth century sugar was still a highly expensive commodity and serving sweet confections was seen as a mark of extravagance and luxury – naturally they featured prominently on the monarch's banquet table.

Inevitably, monarchs that followed Henry VIII needed to update the Hampton Court kitchens, but areas of the original Tudor kitchens have survived and visitors to Hampton Court can still marvel at the facilities available to sixteenth-century cooks.

MINI MERINGUES WITH SUMMER FRUIT AND ELDERFLOWER CREAM

Whether billowing clouds of chewy sweetness or small crunchy rounds, meringues always rise to an occasion, delivering a touch of sophistication. In England, they are commonly served with cream and strawberries in the famous summer dessert, Eton mess. There's no sign of any untidiness in this recipe, however, which would sit proudly on an elegant tea table.

Serves 8
2 large egg whites
around 140g caster sugar

To serve
150ml double cream
1–2 tbsp elderflower cordial
200g summer fruits, such as raspberries, strawberries, blueberries and redcurrants

Preheat the oven to 110°C/gas ¼. Line a large baking sheet with baking parchment and draw eight rounds on top, spaced well apart, using a 6cm glass or cutter. Turn the parchment over so the pen is on the other side.

Weigh the egg whites into a large, spotlessly clean bowl. Note the weight and double it, then measure that quantity of caster sugar into a separate bowl.

Whisk the egg whites for a couple of minutes until they stand in firm peaks. They're ready when you can turn the bowl upside down over your head and the mixture stays exactly where it is.

Whisk in the caster sugar, a tablespoon at a time, making sure that each tablespoon has dissolved into the mixture before adding another. Continue until all the sugar is mixed in.

Spoon the mixture evenly among the outlined rounds, using the back of the spoon to make a dip in the top of each. Bake in the oven for around 1½ hours until a meringue comes away easily from the parchment. Leave in the oven to cool completely with the oven door closed.

Whip the cream and cordial together in a bowl. Arrange the meringues on a platter and spoon the cream into the dips. Decorate with the summer fruit and serve.

THE TOWER OF LONDON

Despite its dour reputation as a menacing prison and place of torture and death, the Tower of London has by far the most unusual and turbulent history of any royal palace and has served its monarchs in the most unexpected ways. From Royal Mint to menagerie, and public record office to protector of priceless jewels, London's iconic fortress is steeped in intrigue, mystery, royal retribution and refuge.

The Tower's story begins with a fight for the English throne. After Edward the Confessor died leaving no successor, his brother-in-law Harold was crowned king, a claim that was challenged by a distant blood relative of Edward's: William, Duke of Normandy. In 1066, William invaded England, fighting and winning the bloody Battle of Hastings to seize the English crown. Realising that he needed to secure his conquest and assert his control over the nation, William set about building an imposing stronghold in London, not only to safeguard the city, but also to strike fear and submission into the hearts of its unruly inhabitants. The White Tower became a mighty mark of the power and prowess of England's new monarch and an enduring symbol of a defining moment in Britain's history.

By 1350, the medieval kings had expanded the fortifications of the White Tower to create the formidable fortress that still stands today. During Henry III's reign (1216–72) the Tower was needed to provide safety and lodging for the monarch during a period of political crisis and war and the nervous young King soon noticed the weakness of the Tower's defences. In 1238 he set about building nine new towers, a massive curtain wall and a moat. His son Edward I continued his defence work, but also began to put the palace to other uses. The minting of coins at the Tower began in 1279, a role it was to hold for more than 500 years.

But it was the coldblooded Henry VIII who really cemented the Tower's reputation as a prison and torture house. Henry's decision to break with the Roman Catholic Church resulted in a wave of religious prisoners being held at the palace. He also executed two of his own wives within its walls. Anne Boleyn's failure to produce an heir saw her accused of adultery and treachery by the King who was anxious to remarry. Just seventeen days after being arrested and locked up in the Tower, Anne was beheaded there by a French swordsman. Henry's fifth wife, young Catherine Howard was also beheaded there, although she was executed in the traditional manner, by axe.

Henry fostered a practice that was to continue right into the twentieth century. First and Second World War spies were condemned to die at the Tower and executions were carried out there until 1941. Yet, despite its inextricable link to the monarchy, the Tower's status as a royal palace came close to being lost during the reign of Charles I (1625–49). Bitter civil war raged between King and Parliament and when the victorious Parliament ordered the execution of the King, the Tower remained in the hands of Oliver Cromwell and his supporters until the monarchy was restored in 1660, the year that also saw the Tower become the permanent home of the Crown Jewels (see pages 40–41).

It was a Victorian fascination with English history that we have to thank for the Tower's appearance today. Nineteenth-century architects were commissioned to restore the palace to its glorious medieval style in order to please the Victorian eye and cater for the increasing number of visitors flocking there. Today, the World Heritage Site continues to honour the Victorian touristic tradition and visitors to the palace can continue to marvel at the splendour of the Crown Jewels, admire the Line of Kings and the suits of armour, pace the fortress walls or try to spot the Tower's famous avian residents.

LEMON AND SULTANA CHEESECAKE

Although in England we tend to think of cheesecake as more of a 'dessert' than a teatime offering, cheesecakes are such a wonderfully decadent and creamy treat that it's hard to see who couldn't fall for a slice as part of a mid-afternoon nibble. What's more, the base in this version, which is scented with lemon and studded with sultanas, is a round of thin sponge, which gives the end result a delicious lightness.

Serves 10–12

500g full-fat cream cheese

150ml double cream

125g golden caster sugar

3 medium eggs, separated

grated zest of 2 lemons

½ tsp vanilla extract

1 tbsp cornflour mixed with the juice of 1 lemon

100g sultanas

For the sponge base

1 medium egg, at room temperature

40g golden caster sugar

grated zest of ½ lemon

40g self-raising flour

15g unsalted butter, melted and cooled, plus extra to grease

Preheat the oven to 170°C/gas 3. Grease and line a 20cm springform cake tin with baking parchment.

Make the sponge base. Whisk the egg and sugar together in a bowl until the mixture has become soft and moussey and leaves a ribbon-like trail when the beaters are lifted.

Fold in the lemon zest, flour and butter very gently using a large metal spoon. Spoon into the tin and bake in the oven for 15 minutes until the cake is golden. Press it lightly in the middle and it should spring back. Allow the sponge to cool in the tin. Leave the oven on.

Beat together the cream cheese, double cream, sugar, egg yolks, lemon zest, vanilla extract and cornflour mixture until thoroughly combined.

Whisk the egg whites in a clean, grease-free bowl until stiff peaks form. Fold one large tablespoon of egg white into the cream cheese mixture to loosen it, then add the remaining egg white and the sultanas and gently fold everything together.

Carefully spoon the mixture into the tin on top of the sponge. Bake in the oven for 45–50 minutes until it's set but still has a slight wobble in the middle. Cool in the tin, then chill overnight before serving. Remove from the fridge 30 minutes to 1 hour before serving to allow the flavours in the cheesecake to develop.

PLUM AND CUSTARD TARTS

Queen Victoria had many things named after during her lifetime, including the fêted sponge cake (see page 24), but the bright red Victoria plum is her only other well-known surviving namesake. Still the most popular type of plum in Britain, Victoria plums have a sweet yet slightly tart flavour, perfect for pairing with a rich custard filling in a pastry case.

Serves 8

For the sweet pastry

120g unsalted butter, softened

50g icing sugar

1 medium egg, beaten

240g plain flour, plus extra for rolling out

a pinch of salt

For the custard filling and plums

2 medium egg yolks

25g caster sugar

1 tbsp cornflour

300ml double cream

seeds from 1 vanilla pod or 2 tsp vanilla extract

4 plums, halved and stoned

2 tbsp light muscovado sugar

a couple of pinches of ground cinnamon

It is said that a Sussex gardener discovered the variety of plum the year Victoria was crowned and named it after her.

For the pastry, beat the butter, sugar and two thirds of the egg together until soft and creamy. If the mixture seems thick, add a little more egg. Stir in the flour and salt until the mixture looks crumbly then bring it together with your hands, kneading lightly to make a smooth dough. Wrap in greaseproof paper and chill for 20 minutes.

Unwrap and divide the chilled pastry into eight then roll out each piece on a lightly floured board and use to line eight 10cm tart tins. Prick each base all over and chill for 15 minutes.

Preheat the oven to 200°C/gas 6 and put in a baking sheet to heat. Line each tin with a piece of crumpled baking parchment and fill with baking beans. Bake in the oven, on the baking sheet, for 10–15 minutes or until the pastry feels dry to the touch. Remove and reduce the oven temperature to 150°C/gas 2.

For the filling, mix the egg yolks, sugar and cornflour together in a bowl. Bring the cream to the boil with the vanilla seeds or extract and stir into the egg yolk mixture. Return the mixture to a clean pan and cook for 1–2 minutes until it thickens slightly. Pour evenly among the tins and bake in the oven for 15–20 minutes, until set, then remove and leave to cool.

Heat an overhead grill. Put the plums cut-side up on a baking sheet and sprinkle with the muscovado sugar and cinnamon, to taste. Grill until golden.

Place a plum half on top of each cooled tart and serve.

BAKEWELL TART

For such a modest bake, Bakewell tart can certainly cause a lot of furore – the pudding-tart debate is very controversial... It is generally accepted that its earliest incarnation, Bakewell Pudding, dates from Tudor times, and was full of rich ingredients that sweet-toothed Henry VIII would have enjoyed. Today, a simple almond filling sits on a layer of jam in the traditional dessert from the town of Bakewell in Derbyshire.

Serves 10–12

For the pastry

175g plain flour, plus extra for rolling out

75g chilled unsalted butter, diced

a pinch of salt

1 medium egg yolk

For the filling

75g unsalted butter, softened

75g golden caster sugar

2 medium eggs

125g ground almonds

25g self-raising flour

¼ tsp almond extract

2–3 tbsp raspberry jam

15g flaked almonds

For the pastry, put the flour, butter and salt into a food processor and whiz until the mixture resembles breadcrumbs. Put the egg yolk in a small bowl and stir in 2 tablespoons of cold water, then add to the breadcrumb mixture and pulse two or three times to mix in the mixture. Tip into a bowl and bring the pastry together with your hands, adding a drizzle more water if the mixture feels dry. Knead the mixture lightly until smooth then shape into a disc, wrap in greaseproof paper and chill for 15 minutes. If you don't have a food processor, rub the butter into the flour lightly using your fingertips. Stir in the egg mixture with a round bladed knife then follow the method above.

Roll the pastry out on a lightly floured board until 2–3mm thick (you may find this easier to do between two sheets of baking parchment) then use to line a 20cm shallow fluted tart tin. Prick the base all over and chill for 15 minutes. Preheat the oven to 190°C/gas 5 and put a baking sheet in to heat too.

Cover the pastry with crumpled baking parchment, fill with baking beans and bake on the preheated sheet for 10 minutes. Lift off the parchment and beans then continue to bake for 5 minutes until the base feels dry. Remove and reduce the oven temperature to 180°C/gas 4.

For the filling, beat together the butter and sugar until creamy, then gradually beat in the eggs. Fold in the ground almonds, flour and almond extract. Spread the jam all over the base of the pastry case then cover with the almond mixture. Sprinkle with flaked almonds and bake in the oven for 30–40 minutes until the filling has turned golden and is firm to the touch.

❋

Purists affirm the original recipe was called a 'pudding' and made with a flaky pastry base, while today it is more commonly made with a crisp shortcrust bottom. Whichever camp you reside in, a small slice is a true teatime treat.

COLONEL BLOOD AND
THE CROWN JEWELS

'Colonel' Thomas Blood was a curious man. He was a
reckless character while also deeply religious, and the
title 'colonel' was in fact self-imposed. He is also the
adventurer at the centre of one of the most mysterious
episodes in the Tower of London's history.

In 1671 Blood began to make frequent visits to the Tower of London and soon befriended the Keeper of the Crown Jewels, Talbot Edwards. For a small fee, the elderly ex-soldier was willing to show visitors the Jewels.

On the morning of 9 May 1671 Blood, and three accomplices, including his son, arrived at the Tower and asked Edwards to show them the jewels. All were secretly armed with knives and pistols, and tied up Edwards and gagged him by ramming a piece of wood in his mouth. The brave old man struggled and was stabbed and clubbed by the cruel thieves. Blood crushed a crown and hid it under his cloak, while one conspirator stuffed the orb down his breeches. But as the thieves were making their escape, Edwards's own son happened upon them and the alarm was raised. After a brief chase the thieves were apprehended.

Unconcerned by his capture, the audacious Blood simply demanded an audience with Charles II. Astonishingly his request was granted. What passed between the King and his insolent subject is unclear, but Blood was subsequently released by royal warrant. What's more, he later received a grant of lands worth over £500 a year. Charles's precise reasons for releasing the traitor may never be known: perhaps he was amused by Blood's daring, but more likely he realised his potential as a valuable spy. Whatever Charles's motives, Blood remains one of the Tower's most intriguing characters, an accolade that sees him commemorated there today – visitors can enjoy a Blood Velvet Cake for afternoon tea (see page 42).

BLOOD VELVET CAKE

When 'Colonel' Thomas Blood tried to steal the Crown Jewels, the Tower of London was almost divested of its most precious treasures. Fortunately, his attempt was thwarted and the Tower's happy triumph over the thief is still commemorated there today with this chocolate-flavoured, blood-red coloured cake. It's finished with a cream cheese icing and a nod to the historic event – chocolate crowns.

Serves 10

100g unsalted butter, softened, plus extra to grease

250g golden caster sugar

2 large eggs, at room temperature

175g plain flour

25g cocoa powder, plus extra to dust

100ml buttermilk

½ tsp bicarbonate of soda

½ tbsp red wine vinegar

1½ tbsp edible red food colouring paste

For the chocolate crowns and icing

50g dark chocolate (minimum 50 per cent cocoa solids), broken into pieces

75g unsalted butter, softened

125g icing sugar

250g cream cheese

Preheat the oven to 180°C/gas 4. Grease and line a deep 16cm round cake tin with greaseproof paper. Whisk together the butter and sugar in a large bowl until soft and creamy. Gradually whisk in the eggs, adding a spoonful of flour if the mixture looks as if it's curdling. Sift over the remaining flour and cocoa powder.

In a separate bowl, mix the buttermilk, bicarbonate of soda, vinegar and food colouring paste together. Add to the flour mixture and fold everything together. Spoon into the tin and bake in the oven for 1 hour 10 minutes, or until a skewer inserted into the centre comes out clean. Remove from the tin and leave to cool on a wire rack.

For the chocolate crowns, put the chocolate into a heatproof bowl, resting over a pan of simmering water. Make sure the bowl doesn't touch the water. As soon as all the chocolate has melted, allow to cool for 5 minutes. Cover a baking sheet with baking parchment. Spoon the chocolate into a small plastic bag, snip the very tip of one of the bag's bottom corners and pipe the shape of crowns by outlining three loops together, a bar underneath and a dot on top of the middle loop for a 'jewel'. Pipe more crowns than you need so you can choose the best shapes. Leave to set at room temperature.

For the icing, beat the butter and icing sugar together, then fold in the cream cheese until smooth. Carefully peel away the paper from the cake and place the cake on a serving plate. Put two large tablespoons of icing aside, then spoon one tablespoon on top of the cake. Smooth it over to cover, then work the mixture around the sides of the cake. Spoon the remaining mixture into a piping bag fitted with a star nozzle and pipe three swirls in the centre of the cake. Push a chocolate crown into each and serve.

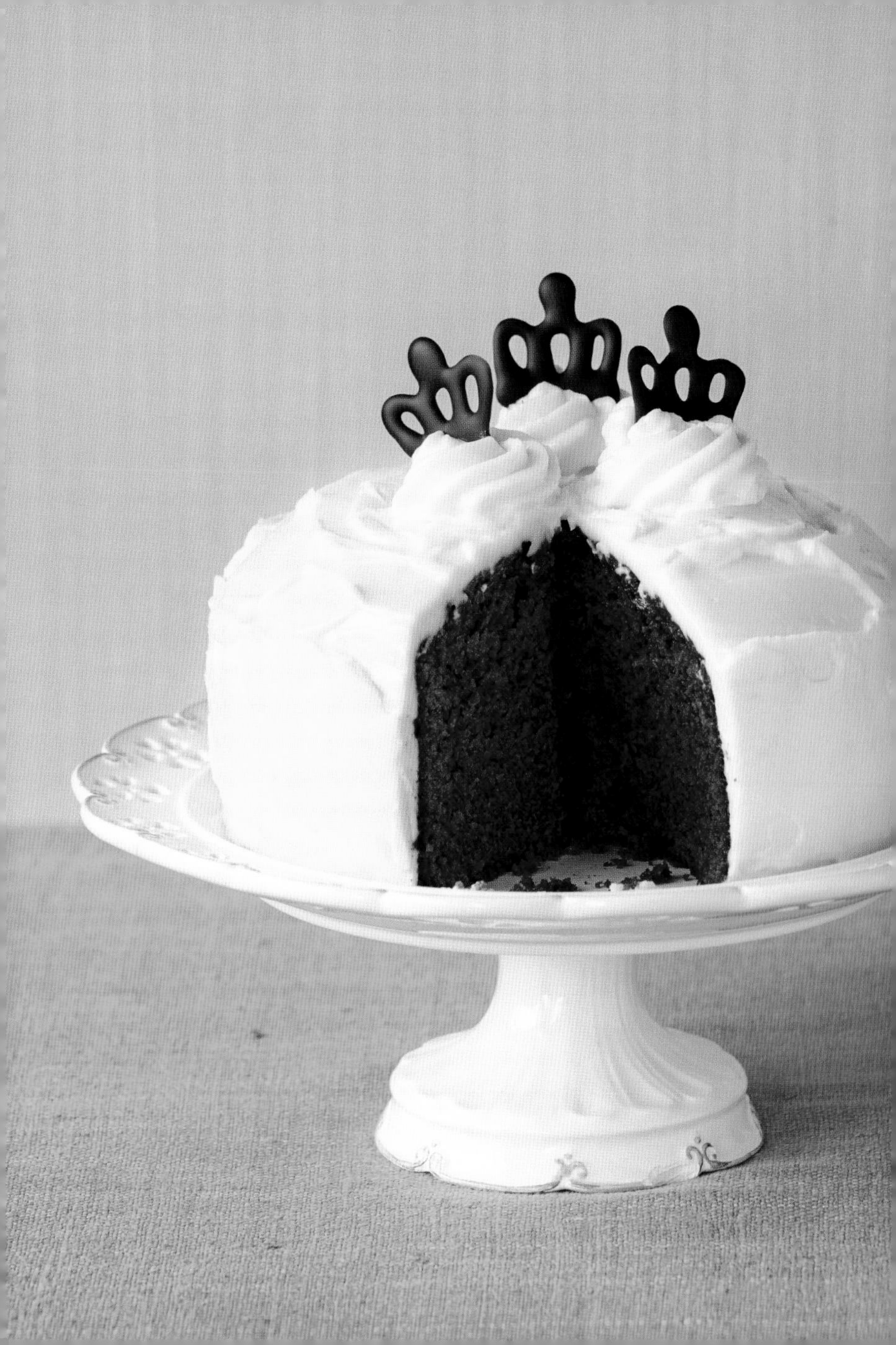

ORANGE MERINGUE TARTLETS

Basing these on the classic English dessert, lemon meringue pie,
we've swapped the lemons for a tart orange curd that sits
inside crisp sweet pastry and is crowned with a dollop
of soft meringue.

Makes 6

250g ready-made sweet
shortcrust pastry

30g cornflour, plus 1 tsp

150ml water

120g golden caster sugar

grated zest and juice of
2 oranges

1 large egg, separated

Roll the pastry out on a lightly floured board until
2–3mm thick (you may find this easier to do between
two sheets of baking parchment) then use to line six
10cm fluted tart tins. Prick the bases all over and chill
for 15 minutes. Preheat the oven to 190°C/gas 5 and
put a baking sheet in to heat too.

Cover each tartlet tin with crumpled baking parchment
then fill with baking beans. Bake the pastry cases on
the preheated baking sheet for 10 minutes then lift
off the paper and beans and continue to bake for a
further 5 minutes, until the base feels dry to the touch.
Remove and reduce the oven temperature to 180°C/
gas 4.

Put the 30g of cornflour, water and 40g of the caster
sugar into a pan and heat gently to dissolve the sugar.
Take the pan off the heat and stir in the orange zest,
juice and egg yolk. Give it a good beat, then return the
pan to the heat and continue to cook until the mixture
has thickened. Remove the pan from the heat.

Whisk the egg white in a spotlessly clean grease-free
bowl until the mixture stands in soft peaks. Gradually
whisk in the remaining caster sugar until combined
then whisk in the teaspoon of cornflour.

Divide the orange mixture evenly between the tart tins
then spoon the meringue on top. Bake in the oven for
around 10–12 minutes until very pale golden all over.

DARK CHOCOLATE SQUARES

There's no doubt that chocolate is a favourite ingredient in the royal household. Both Prince William and his grandmother are partial to a slice of chocolate fridge cake (see page 72 for the recipe), while the Queen's 80th birthday cake was a rich chocolate sponge. So our dainty little cocoa squares are a teatime treat truly fit for a queen.

Makes 25

150g unsalted butter, chopped, plus extra to grease

200g dark chocolate (minimum 50 per cent cocoa solids), finely chopped

175g golden caster sugar

2 large eggs

175g self-raising flour

25g cocoa powder

To decorate

150ml double cream

1 tbsp icing sugar

raspberries

Preheat the oven to 190°C/gas 5. Grease and line a 19cm square cake tin with baking parchment.

Melt the butter and 150g of the chocolate in a pan over a low heat. Carefully mix together then set aside to cool a little.

Whisk the sugar and eggs together in a bowl using an electric hand whisk until the mixture is moussey and falls in thick ribbons when the whisks are lifted.

Sift over the flour and cocoa powder then add the melted chocolate mixture along with the remaining chopped chocolate. Fold everything together carefully using a large metal spoon.

Bake in the oven for 30 minutes until firm. Cool in the tin for 10 minutes then transfer to a wire rack to cool completely.

To serve, whip the double cream with the icing sugar until just firm. Cut the cake into 25 squares and spoon a little whipped cream on top of each. Top each with a raspberry.

COFFEE ÉCLAIRS

Though éclairs are thought to have originated in France at the turn of the nineteenth century where they were created for French royalty, they now take pride of place on English afternoon tea tables. The little oblongs of crisp choux pastry are filled with either a cream or custardy filling and topped with icing or melted chocolate. Fill them as soon as they've cooled and enjoy them on the day they're made for the best crisp bite.

Makes 6

25g unsalted butter

40g plain flour, sifted three times

1 medium egg

150ml double cream

½ tsp espresso coffee powder

1 tsp golden icing sugar

For the topping

4 tbsp fondant icing sugar

1 tsp cocoa powder

Preheat the oven to 220°C/gas 7. Lightly grease a baking sheet and sprinkle with water.

Place the butter in a small pan with 75ml water over a low heat. When the butter has melted, increase the heat slightly to bring the liquid to a rolling boil. Remove the pan from the heat and stir in the flour. Beat furiously with a wooden spoon over the heat again until the mixture forms a ball and comes away clean from the sides of the pan.

Spoon into a bowl and allow the mixture to cool a little. Gradually beat in the egg until the mixture is smooth and shiny, and a spoonful falls easily from the spoon.

Spoon into a piping bag fitted with a 1cm round nozzle. Pipe six lengths of mixture, around 8–10cm each, on to the baking sheet. Bake in the oven for 10–15 minutes until golden. Carefully push a knife into the side of each then return to the oven for 1–2 minutes to allow the inside to cook. Transfer to a wire rack to cool completely.

Whip the double cream, espresso powder and icing sugar until thick. Pipe or spoon into each éclair.

For the topping, mix the fondant icing sugar with the cocoa powder and 1 teaspoon of water, until it's the consistency of toothpaste. Spoon over the top of each éclair and allow to set before serving.

TEA BREADS,
BUNS
AND
BISCUITS

FRUIT TEACAKES

Teacakes are simple, soft sweet buns that are traditionally served toasted, with lashings of butter, accompanied by a pot of tea. We think our more luxurious version, filled with flaked almonds and preserved ginger and scented with orange, transforms the humble teacake to make it fit enough for a queen.

Makes 12

1 x 7g sachet dried yeast

50g golden caster sugar

325–375ml warm milk

500g strong plain bread flour

1 tsp ground mixed spice

50g dried cranberries

25g flaked almonds

40g mixed peel

25g preserved ginger, chopped

grated zest of ½ orange

¼ tsp salt

1 medium egg, beaten, plus 1 egg yolk

a little vegetable oil, for greasing

1 tbsp demerara sugar

Put the yeast and 1 teaspoon of the caster sugar into a bowl and pour in 100ml of the milk. Stir together and set aside for 10 minutes to activate the yeast.

Sift the flour and mixed spice into a large bowl and stir in the cranberries, almonds, peel, ginger, orange zest and salt. Toss together. Make a well in the middle and pour in 225ml more milk, the whole egg and the yeast mixture. Stir everything together with a knife to make a craggy dough. If the dough seems dry, add the rest of the milk.

Knead on a board until smooth and elastic. Alternatively do this in a freestanding mixer. Put in a lightly oiled bowl, cover and leave to prove for around 1 hour, until doubled in size.

Divide the dough into 12 and roll each piece into a round. Place on a lightly oiled baking sheet. Set aside in a draught-free place to rise for 30 minutes.

Preheat the oven to 190°C/gas 5. Bake in the oven for 20 minutes. Beat the egg yolk with 1 tablespoon of cold water and use to glaze the buns. Sprinkle with the demerara sugar then return to the oven for 5–10 minutes until golden and the bases sound hollow when tapped. Serve warm or slice and toast with butter. Store in an airtight container for up to four days.

GINGER, PEAR AND SULTANA LOAF CAKE

Although this fruity cake can be made at any time of year, in Britain it's best enjoyed in autumn when British pears are in season and at their best. The soothing pairing of sweet pear and warming ginger makes it the perfect slice to revive and restore you after a long walk on a cold autumnal afternoon.

Serves 10

2 small ripe pears

100g unsalted butter, softened

125g soft light brown sugar

2 tbsp stem ginger syrup, plus extra to glaze

2 eggs, beaten

150g self-raising flour

125g wholemeal self-raising flour

50g finely chopped hazelnuts

1 tsp ground ginger

50g sultanas

2 balls stem ginger (in syrup), grated or finely chopped

125ml milk

Preheat the oven to 180°C/gas 4. Line a 900g loaf tin with a cake liner or baking parchment.

Chop 1½ pears, removing the stalk, core and any seeds. Set aside.

Cream the butter, sugar and ginger syrup together in a large bowl. Quickly beat in the eggs, then fold in both flours, hazelnuts and ground ginger.

Add the chopped pears, sultanas, stem ginger and milk and fold in to make a thick batter.

Spoon into the prepared tin and level the top. Remove the core from the remaining pear half, then slice lengthways. Arrange on top of the cake. Bake in the oven for 1–1¼ hours until the cake is golden.

Brush 1–2 tablespoons of stem ginger syrup over the cake and leave to cool in the tin for 20 minutes, then transfer to a wire rack to cool completely.

KENSINGTON PALACE

A stroll through one of London's most famous parks brings you to the immaculately-manicured lawns of Kensington Gardens, and within them the arresting red-brick façade of Kensington Palace.

Given its situation in the heart of central London, it's hard to imagine that where Kensington Palace stands today was once a remote village. William III and Mary II (1689–1702) bought what was then Nottingham House in 1689 to provide them with a retreat from the 'grime' of Whitehall Palace. Within weeks, Sir Christopher Wren had been appointed to set about improving the house, transforming it into a series of grand rooms – the State Apartments; a suitable setting for the royal court. And so began Kensington's life as a royal residence.

Despite her short reign, William and Mary's successor, Queen Anne, remains famous in the life of Kensington; her legacy being the striking Orangery (see pages 68–9), built in 1704–5. Originally designed as a greenhouse for Anne's citrus trees, the Orangery was also used as a stunning venue for balls and soirées. And today, the Orangery continues to honour its role as a setting for ceremony, as a place where visitors can come to enjoy a traditional afternoon tea.

Scenes of love, loss, happiness and heartbreak have played out within Kensington's walls. Its period of prominence during the reign of George II and Queen Caroline saw it sparkling and humming with the sounds of laughter and lavish entertainment. It was here that the young Princess, later Queen, Victoria was brought up, educated under the strict 'Kensington System' and where she rode her pony Rosie in the park. More famously, it is where she first set eyes upon her beloved Albert. In more recent times, it has been the birthplace and home of future monarchs. Diana lived here until her death in 1997; both Princes William and Harry, spent their formative years here; and William has returned to live here with Catherine and their son George. For despite all its grandeur, exquisite décor and spaces open to the public, part of Kensington Palace is still a royal home.

DATE AND WALNUT TEA BREAD

The late Queen Elizabeth the Queen Mother is thought to have been rather fond of this classic combination and enjoyed date and walnut cake for her afternoon tea. Our version is in fact a tea bread – we've soaked the dates in tea as is traditional for a tea bread, which keeps the loaf wonderfully moist. It's finished with a moreish icing made with whisky, cream and butter.

Serves 10

200g dried dates, chopped

150ml freshly brewed Earl Grey tea

50g unsalted butter, softened

½ tsp bicarbonate of soda

75g light muscovado sugar

225g self-raising flour, sifted

2 large eggs, beaten

75g walnuts, roughly chopped

For the icing

25g light muscovado sugar

20g icing sugar

2 tbsp whisky

30g unsalted butter, softened

2 tbsp double cream

20g walnuts, roughly chopped

Preheat the oven to 170°C/gas 3. Line a 900g loaf tin with a cake liner or baking parchment.

Put the dates in a large bowl, pour over the tea then stir in the butter. Leave to soak for at least an hour.

Add the remaining ingredients and stir thoroughly to ensure everything is well combined. Spoon into the tin and bake in the oven for 1 hour or until a skewer inserted into the centre comes out clean. Cool in the tin for 10 minutes, then transfer to a wire rack to cool completely.

To make the icing, put the sugars and whisky in a small pan and bring to the boil. Simmer for 1–2 minutes to cook off the alcohol then take the pan off the heat and set aside to cool. Once cool, beat the butter and cream into the syrup to make an icing. Spread over the cake then scatter the chopped walnuts over the top. The cake will keep in an airtight container for up to five days.

CHELSEA BUNS

This recipe dates back to the eighteenth century and was created in a London establishment called the Chelsea Bun House, thought to have been patronised by King George II and III. Sticky, fruity and very sweet, the dough is rolled up like a blanket then sliced into buns.

Makes 12

1 x 7g sachet dried yeast

50g golden caster sugar

300ml warm milk

500g strong plain bread flour

1 tsp ground mixed spice

¼ tsp salt

75g unsalted butter, softened, plus extra to grease

1 medium egg, beaten

a little vegetable oil, for greasing

15g demerara sugar, plus extra to finish

grated zest of ½ lemon

75g currants

75g sultanas

apricot jam, to finish

Line a large roasting tin with baking parchment. Put the yeast and 1 teaspoon of the caster sugar into a bowl and pour in 100ml of the warm milk. Stir and set aside for 10 minutes to activate the yeast.

Sift the flour, mixed spice and salt into a large bowl. Rub in 25g of the butter using your fingertips. Make a well in the middle of the mixture and pour in the yeast mix, remaining milk and egg. Stir the ingredients with a knife until it comes together into a rough dough, then knead on a board until smooth.

Place in a clean, oiled bowl and cover. Leave to prove for around 1 hour, until the dough has doubled in size. Place the dough on a board and knead two to three times to knock back. Roll out on a large board until the mixture measures around 36 x 30cm.

Beat the remaining butter, demerara sugar and lemon zest together in a bowl until smooth. Spread all over the dough then sprinkle with the dried fruit, pressing it down lightly so it sticks to the butter.

With the longest side facing you, roll the dough up, then cut into 12 rolls and place in the roasting tin. Cover and leave to prove for 30 minutes in a draught-free place. Preheat the oven to 190°C/gas 5.

Uncover the tin, transfer to the oven and bake for 20–25 minutes until the buns are golden. Brush with the jam and return to the oven for 5 minutes to set.

Cool in the tin for 5 minutes, then transfer to a wire rack to cool completely. Break into individual rolls and serve. Store in an airtight container for up to two days.

Sugary buns have been enjoyed in Britain since around the fifteenth century and many are named after the place they originated.

LEMON CURD BISCUITS

This two-in-one recipe creates not just a batch of zesty bite-sized biscuits, it also makes a small jar of lemon curd, which is lovely served on a homemade scone (see page 70).

Makes around 22

100g unsalted butter, softened

40g granulated sugar

40g soft light brown sugar

½ tsp vanilla extract

a good pinch of salt

grated zest of 1 lemon

175g plain flour

For the lemon curd

1 large egg

30g unsalted butter

50g caster sugar

juice of ½ lemon

Start by making the lemon curd. Put the egg, butter, sugar and lemon juice in a bowl set over a pan of simmering water (make sure the base of the bowl isn't touching the water). Allow the butter to melt and stir all the ingredients together. Cook for a further 10 minutes until the mixture has thickened. Strain into a separate bowl and allow to cool.

Preheat the oven to 190°C/gas 5. Line two baking sheets with baking parchment.

For the biscuits, beat the butter, sugars, vanilla extract, salt and lemon zest together in a large bowl until soft and creamy. Stir in 40g of the lemon curd (spoon any left over into a sterilised sealable pot and chill; use within a week).

Work in the flour to make a thick dough. Use a teaspoon to take a small scoop of the mixture then scrape it on to the baking sheet and flatten each slightly.

Bake in the oven for around 15 minutes until golden. Store in an airtight tin for up to five days.

ALL-BUTTER ALMOND SHORTBREAD

The refinement of this crumbly Scottish biscuit is often credited to Mary Queen of Scots, who is said to have been partial to petticoat tails – the traditional triangular-shape in which shortbread is often served. Why they are called petticoat tails is something of a mystery – most likely is the theory that they resembled 'petticoat tallies', the word for the pattern used to make the bell hoop petticoats worn by Elizabeth I.

Makes 8

125g unsalted butter, softened, plus extra to grease

50g golden caster sugar, plus extra to dust

100g plain flour

50g cornflour

25g ground almonds

Preheat the oven to 150°C/gas 2. Lightly grease a round 17cm tin.

Using a wooden spoon, beat the butter and sugar together in a large bowl until soft and creamy.

Sift in the flour and cornflour, then add the ground almonds to the bowl. Work the dry ingredients into the butter mixture using the back of the spoon to make a dough. Spoon the mixture into the tin then press it down using the back of the spoon to smooth the top.

Press the tip of a table knife all around the edge of the shortbread to emboss the round end onto the pastry and create a pattern, then score into eight triangles. Prick the triangles all over with a fork.

Transfer to the oven and bake for 30 minutes. Remove the tray from the oven and score the triangles again then continue to bake for a further 30–40 minutes until set and golden around the edges. Dust with extra sugar and leave in the tin to cool completely.

Cut down the edges of each triangle with a sharp knife to remove each piece. Store in an airtight tin for up to five days.

ORANGE BISCUITS WITH CHOCOLATE CHIPS

Dark chocolate is paired with its tried and trusted partner, orange, to make a lovely rounded little biscuit that's perfect at any time of the day. It's important to plump for a dark chocolate with a high cocoa percentage, though, to make sure the biscuits aren't too sweet.

Makes around 25–30

125g unsalted butter, softened

50g golden granulated sugar

50g soft light brown sugar

1 medium egg, beaten

½ tsp vanilla extract

a good pinch of salt

175g plain flour

grated zest of 1 orange

75g dark chocolate (70 per cent cocoa solids), roughly chopped or use chocolate chips

Preheat the oven to 190°C/gas 5. Line two baking sheets with baking parchment.

Put the butter and the sugars into a large bowl and cream together using an electric hand whisk. Quickly whisk in the egg, vanilla extract and salt, scraping down the sides of the bowl.

Add the flour, orange zest and chocolate and fold together using a wooden spoon to make a soft dough.

Take teaspoonfuls of the mixture and roll them into rounds. Place on the baking sheet and flatten slightly. Bake in the oven for around 15 minutes, until just golden round the edges. Store in an airtight tin for up to five days.

SULTANA AND SPICE BISCUITS

In Britain, it's thought that no problem can't be solved if you sit down and have a cup of tea and a biscuit. These gently spiced butter biscuits, with their crunchy sugar topping and juicy sultanas, are a deliciously moreish accompaniment to your afternoon brew – perfect for putting the world to rights. They're particularly good with a cup of Earl Grey tea.

Makes 26

150g unsalted butter, softened

75g golden caster sugar

1 tsp ground mixed spice

grated zest of 1 small orange

175g plain flour, plus extra to dust

50g sultanas

Preheat the oven to 180°C/gas 4. Line two baking sheets with baking parchment.

Cream the butter, sugar, mixed spice and orange zest together in a bowl with a wooden spoon until the mixture looks creamy and the sugar has started to dissolve.

Sift over the flour and add the sultanas to the bowl, too. Work the mixture thoroughly, using the back of the wooden spoon to mix everything together. Knead briefly with your hands to make the dough smooth. Wrap in greaseproof paper and chill for 20 minutes.

Lightly flour a clean work surface and roll out the dough until it is 3–4mm thick.

Stamp out rounds using a 6cm round or fluted cutter. Transfer to the lined baking sheets and chill again for 15 minutes. Bake in the oven for 12–15 minutes, until just starting to turn golden round the edges. Sprinkle with a little extra sugar, then transfer to a wire rack to cool. Store in an airtight tin for up to five days.

QUEEN ANNE AND
HER ORANGERY

Historians can often be unkind about this somewhat
rotund royal who is often best remembered for what
she didn't achieve, rather than what she did.

Tragic Queen Anne (1702–14) was pregnant 17 times, but only five babies survived full term. Of the five babies only one lived beyond infancy – her son, William of Gloucester, who died at the age of 11. Yet while she is also responsible for the significant achievement of uniting England and Scotland, visitors to Kensington Palace will be able to behold her more elegant and still remarkable legacy to its gardens.

In 1704, Anne requested that substantial sums of Treasury money be spent on designing and building her an orangery in which she could grow a collection of exotic citrus trees. The result of the project, which was fraught with controversy and exceeded its already considerable budget three times over, is arguably one of London's most attractive buildings and Anne was delighted with it. Her Orangery became a haven for her: she hosted lavish parties there and sat on the terrace enjoying the view of her beloved gardens.

The Orangery still serves as a setting for entertainment and serenity. Visitors can enjoy a sumptuous traditional afternoon tea in the light-filled, airy room, and Queen Anne herself is even commemorated in the style of scone that is served: orange-scented currant scones (see recipe overleaf), while the Orangery continues to play host to summer parties.

ORANGE-SCENTED CURRANT SCONES

These delightful fruity scones are the ones you will find served for afternoon tea at The Orangery at Kensington Palace. The recipe pays tribute to Queen Anne, who built the magnificent glass structure to house her collection of citrus trees. Serve them in true British style – with clotted cream and jam.

Makes 8

225g self-raising flour

50g chilled unsalted butter, cubed

2 tbsp golden caster sugar

grated zest of 1 orange

50g currants

100ml buttermilk

50–75ml milk, plus extra for brushing

To serve

clotted cream

jam

Preheat the oven to 220°C/gas 7. Line a baking sheet with baking parchment.

Sift the flour into a large bowl. Rub the butter into the flour using your fingertips until the mixture resembles breadcrumbs. Stir in the caster sugar, orange zest and currants.

Make a well in the centre and pour in the buttermilk and milk. Use a round-bladed knife to stir everything together to make a rough dough. Bring it together with your hands then tip it gently on to a board and knead it lightly and quickly until the dough is smooth.

Pat down and shape into a round about 2.5cm thick. Cut out rounds using a 6cm cutter, re-rolling the dough as necessary, then place on the prepared baking sheet. Brush with a little milk and bake in the oven for 15 minutes, until just golden, then remove from the oven and transfer to a wire rack to cool. Serve with clotted cream and jam. Store in an airtight container for up to three days.

CHOCOLATE FRIDGE CAKE

There are many variations of this rich chocolatey cake, which is so simple to make because it is set in the fridge rather than being baked. Our recipe is based on the version thought to be Prince William's favoured childhood treat.

Serves 12

150g unsalted butter, plus extra to grease

100g golden syrup

300g dark chocolate (minimum 50 per cent cocoa solids), chopped

1 tbsp brandy

200g Rich Tea or digestive biscuits

Grease and line a deep 16cm round cake tin with baking parchment.

Melt the butter in a pan with the syrup and 125g of the chocolate. As soon as all the ingredients have melted, stir in the brandy. Heat for 1 minute, then take the pan off the heat.

Use a large chopping knife to crush the biscuits, in batches, into bite-sized chunks. Make sure they're not too big otherwise the chocolate mixture won't coat the biscuits properly, or too small, which will make the texture dense.

Stir the biscuits into the chocolate mixture, ensuring they're all coated. Spoon into the lined tin, making sure there aren't any holes. Chill in the fridge for one hour or until firm.

Remove the cake from the tin and place on a rack, resting over a tray lined with baking parchment. Melt the remaining chocolate in a bowl set over a pan of simmering water, making sure the base of the bowl doesn't touch the water. Allow to cool for 10 minutes, then spoon all over the cake, ensuring the sides are covered. Cool at room temperature, then serve in thin slices. Store in an airtight container for up to five days.

So great is his fondness for fridge cake that at his wedding Prince William revived a great Victorian tradition and requested to have a 'groom's cake' alongside the traditional fruit cake.

JAM PENNIES

Afternoon tea is still served in today's royal household every day when the monarch is not banqueting and these miniature jam sandwiches are said to be a particular favourite of Queen Elizabeth II. So simple to prepare, they provide the perfect afternoon pick-me-up.

Serves 4

8 slices white bread

a little softened butter

strawberry or raspberry jam

Use a 4–5cm round cutter to cut out three circles from each slice of bread. Spread a little butter over each piece.

Spoon about half a teaspoon of jam on to 12 rounds, spread it just to the edge then top with the other rounds of bread and press lightly together to secure.

SANDWICHES
AND
SAVOURIES

CUCUMBER AND MINT SANDWICHES

Finger sandwiches are an essential element of a traditional afternoon tea – delicate little savoury morsels to start the meal. Serve them as they are still served to Queen Elizabeth today – with the crusts removed.

Makes 3 fingers

4 thin slices peeled cucumber

2 mint leaves, finely chopped

1 tsp white wine vinegar

1 tsp olive oil

softened butter

1 slice brown bread

1 slice white bread

Marinate the cucumber in a bowl with the mint, vinegar and olive oil for 10 minutes.

Spread each slice of bread with butter, then lay the slices of cucumber on top of one half. Put the other slice of bread on top and press to secure. Slice off the crusts, cut the sandwich into three fingers and serve.

As Edwardian court ladies were never invited to lunch in one of the new-fangled restaurants, they made tea their own, changing into loose 'tea gowns' that allowed them to remove their tightly-laced stays and relax as they sipped and munched on delicious cakes, macaroons and crumpets. But by 8.30pm they would have to be laced up tightly again and appear in tiaras and evening gowns, ready for a 12-course dinner.

HONEY-ROASTED HAM WITH ENGLISH MUSTARD SANDWICHES

Makes 3 fingers

2 tsp unsalted butter, softened

1 tsp English mustard

2 slices white bread

1 slice ham

Beat the butter and mustard together in a small bowl then spread half over each slice of bread. Arrange the ham over one slice, then put the other slice of bread on top and press to secure. Slice off the crusts, cut the sandwich into three fingers and serve.

THINLY SLICED TOMATO AND GENTLEMEN'S RELISH SANDWICHES

Makes 3 fingers

2 tsp gentlemen's relish

2 slices white bread

½ tomato, sliced

Spread the gentlemen's relish over the slices of bread. Arrange the tomato slices over one slice, then put the other slice of bread on top and press to secure. Slice off the crusts, cut the sandwich into three fingers and serve.

SMOKED SALMON SANDWICHES

Makes 3 fingers

2 tsp unsalted butter, softened

1 tsp chopped herbs, such as chives and parsley

a squeeze of lemon juice

2 slices brown bread

2 slices smoked salmon

salt and freshly ground white pepper

Beat the butter, herbs, lemon juice and seasoning together in a bowl. Spread over each slice of bread then top one half with the smoked salmon. Put the other slice of bread on top and press lightly to secure. Slice off the crusts, cut the sandwich into three fingers and serve.

EGG MAYONNAISE SANDWICHES

Makes 3 fingers

1 hard-boiled egg

2–3 tbsp mayonnaise

1 tbsp chopped chives

softened butter

1 slice brown bread

1 slice white bread

salt and freshly ground black pepper

Mash the egg, mayonnaise and chives together in a bowl with some seasoning. Spread butter over one slice of bread and spoon over the egg mixture, smoothing it out just to the edges. Put the other slice of bread on top and press lightly to secure. Slice off the crusts, cut the sandwich into three fingers and serve.

CURED DILL SALMON AND BEETROOT BLINIS

Blinis are fluffy savoury pancakes. The tangy flavour of the little rounds is a perfect vehicle for smoked fish and other similar delicacies so they're a lovely morsel to nibble on at the start of an afternoon tea or cocktail party, preferably with a glass of champagne. In this recipe, slivers of home-cured salmon sit majestically on blinis, garnished with crème fraîche and jewels of diced beetroot.

Serves 6

For the cured salmon

300g salmon fillet, with skin

2 tbsp chopped dill

1 tsp salt

1 tbsp golden caster sugar

½ tsp ground white pepper

grated zest of ½ lemon

For the blinis

1 tsp dried yeast

100g buckwheat flour

25g plain flour

½ tsp caster sugar

150ml milk

15g unsalted butter, melted and cooled

1 medium egg, separated

a pinch of salt

sunflower oil, for frying

To garnish

crème fraîche

2 ready-cooked beetroot, cut into small dice

dill sprigs

Put the salmon on a piece of cling film, skin-side down. Mix together the remaining cure ingredients and spoon over the fish, then wrap tightly in the cling film. Turn the salmon over so the skin is uppermost and put in a small container. Place a heavy weight on top and chill for three days.

For the blinis, put the yeast, flours, sugar, milk, butter and egg yolk in a bowl and whisk together. Cover and set aside for 30 minutes. Whisk the egg white in a clean bowl until the mixture stands in soft peaks. Fold into the flour mixture with a pinch of salt.

Heat a teaspoon of oil in a pan. Use a dessertspoon to spoon small mounds of the blini batter into the pan. Shape into 7cm rounds and allow to cook for a few minutes on each side until golden brown. Continue to cook the blinis in batches, adding more oil to the pan as necessary, until you've used up all the mixture.

Slice the cured salmon into thin slivers and place on top of each blini. Spoon over a little crème fraîche and top with a little beetroot and a sprig of dill. Serve straight away. There'll be some leftover salmon, which keeps well, wrapped in cling film, in the fridge for another two days.

TOASTS WITH CURED BEEF AND MUSTARD MAYONNAISE

This recipe for a simple cure infuses tender beef fillet with a punchy peppery flavour. We've mixed the accompanying mustard with mayonnaise so as not to overpower the wonderfully flavoursome beef, but if you're a stickler for tradition, serve it with a tangy English mustard.

Serves 6

½ tsp mixed peppercorns

a good pinch of cayenne pepper

½ tsp fennel seeds

1 tsp salt

150g trimmed beef fillet

olive oil, for frying

4 tbsp mayonnaise

1 tsp Dijon mustard

1 tsp chopped tarragon, plus extra sprigs to garnish

12 slices baguette, toasted

6 gherkins, halved

Grind the peppercorns, cayenne, fennel seeds and salt together in a pestle and mortar or small spice grinder until finely ground. Put the beef fillet on a piece of cling film and rub the spice mix all over. Wrap tightly in the cling film and chill in the fridge for up to three days.

To cook the beef, heat a little olive oil in a frying pan, unwrap the beef and brown it on all sides. Set aside on a board to cool.

Mix together the mayonnaise, mustard and tarragon. If it seems very thick, stir in 1–2 teaspoons of cold water. Spread a little on each slice of toast. Slice the beef thinly and arrange on top. Garnish with a gherkin half and serve with a sprig of tarragon. There'll be some leftover beef, which keeps well, wrapped in cling film, in the fridge for another two days.

Curing meat by packing it in salt and other aromatics is one of the most ancient forms of food preservation and flavouring. It would certainly have come in handy in Tudor times when refrigeration was unknown and vast quantities of meat were needed to satisfy Henry VIII's voracious appetite. While the average Tudor family lived on vegetables, with the occasional bit of preserved meat, Henry and his most senior courtiers would expect a predominantly meat-based diet. Dishes of spit-roasted beef or mutton and stews of pork and chicken were supplied in plenty. Along with these more familiar meats, there were many animals and particularly birds that would not feature on a menu today, including peacock, heron and swan!

KEW PALACE

Nestled among magnificent botanical gardens on the banks of the River Thames, is the smallest and most intimate of English palaces. George II and his wife Caroline acquired the striking double-fronted villa (known as the Dutch House) in 1729, as a residence for their three daughters. They established a tradition that was to prevail throughout Kew's royal occupancy, that of a family home. The villa was one of several properties around Kew and their son, Prince Frederick, refurbished another just opposite the palatial White House, which no longer survives.

Frederick and his wife Augusta were horticultural enthusiasts and visitors today enjoy one of Kew's most remarkable and loved attractions – its beautiful gardens – thanks to their passion. The couple landscaped, designed and laid the foundations for the botanic gardens. Tragedy struck when Frederick suffered an untimely death, however, Augusta was to continue their work alone. Strolling in the gardens today visitors will still encounter Augusta's devotion to her craft: the ornate Japanese pagoda and follies as well as her enchanting Physic Garden and medicinal plantings.

George III (1760–1820) spent much of his childhood at Kew Palace and from 1781 to 1818 he moved into the White House with his wife Charlotte and their 15 children. A loving father and devoted husband, George III turned Kew into a happy family home. Until the King's illness, its rooms rang with laughter, fun and celebration, and it became a refuge where the young family could enjoy a simple domestic routine away from the spotlight of public life.

At the very bottom of the gardens, Queen Charlotte built herself a tiny thatched cottage. It was designed as a rustic retreat, where she and her family could retire, take tea and enjoy a favourite pastime, picnicking together among the tranquil greenery of the gardens. The cottage also overlooked a small menagerie, home to pheasants and other exotic birds but also to kangaroos, which must have delighted the royal children.

Today, many of the grand historic buildings that graced the Gardens, including a castellated palace, are gone, but the charming cottage, the surprising Georgian kitchens, the Orangery, Pagoda and the diminutive Kew Palace still survive for us all to enjoy. In 2006 Kew Palace was once again to play host to a family occasion. Prince Charles opened the doors of George III's dining room for a surprise dinner party for his mother, a private celebration in honour of the Queen's 80th birthday. The immediate Royal Family enjoyed the smoked salmon, venison and chocolate sponge; a far richer meal than many of those partaken by the famously health-conscious George III, who avoided alcohol and was known to heartily recommend a simple boiled egg for supper!

CORONATION CHICKEN
FINGER ROLLS

Originally called 'Chicken Elizabeth' this recipe was invented by Constance Spry and Rosemary Hume, the principals of the Cordon Bleu Cookery School, and was developed for Queen Elizabeth II's coronation in 1953. With tender chunks of chicken coated in a mildly-spiced sauce with mayonnaise, the dish was deemed to have the appropriate combination of luxury and austerity at a time when the country was still experiencing post-war rationing.

Serves 6

For the rolls

½ tsp dried yeast

a pinch of sugar

150g strong wholemeal flour

50g strong plain flour

15g unsalted butter, cubed

a good pinch of salt

For the coronation chicken

1 tsp curry powder

4 tbsp mayonnaise

1 tsp crème fraîche

1½ tbsp mango chutney

100g roast chicken, shredded

sprigs of watercress

salt and freshly ground black pepper

Put the yeast in a bowl with the sugar. Add 1 tablespoon of warm water and set aside to allow the yeast to activate.

Sift the flours into a bowl and rub in the butter and salt with your fingertips. Make a well in the middle and pour in the yeast mixture, along with 125–150ml warm water. Mix well then knead on a board to make a soft sticky dough. Place in a clean bowl, cover and allow to rise for 30 minutes in a warm place.

Divide the dough into six and shape each one into a finger roll. Put on a baking sheet lined with baking parchment and leave to prove for 30 minutes. Preheat the oven to 190°C/gas 5.

Bake the rolls for 15–20 minutes until golden and the base sounds hollow when tapped. Cool on a wire rack.

For the chicken, put the curry powder in a pan and heat for a minute or two until you can smell the aroma of the spices. Tip into a bowl and add the mayonnaise, crème fraiche, chutney and plenty of seasoning. Stir in the chicken. If the mixture is very thick, stir in 1–2 teaspoons of water.

Slice the rolls in half. Spoon a little coronation chicken on to the bottom of each, top with watercress then rest the roll on top and serve.

SMOKED MACKEREL PÂTÉ AND CAPERS ON TOAST

Smoked mackerel can be quite a strong flavour but mixing it with mild cheese and mayonnaise mellows it and creates a deliciously creamy spread for little triangles of thin toast. Adjust the lemon juice and paprika according to your taste.

Serves 6

100g smoked mackerel fillet

1 tbsp cream cheese

1 tbsp mayonnaise

juice of ½ lemon

½ tsp paprika

salt and freshly ground black pepper

To serve

5 slices granary bread

caper berries

parsley sprigs, to garnish (optional)

Break up the smoked mackerel fillet, taking care to remove any bones. Put the pieces into a small food processor with the cream cheese, mayonnaise, lemon juice and paprika. Season with a pinch of salt and plenty of pepper. Whizz to make a smooth pâté then check the seasoning and adjust accordingly.

To serve, toast the bread then take a sharp bread knife and cut off all the crusts of each piece to make a square. Take a slice and carefully cut it horizontally – between the toasted sides – to make two thin slices. Cut each of these into two triangles then grill the untoasted sides.

Do the same with the other pieces of toast until you've made 18 triangles (serve three each and there'll be two pieces left over out of which you can make breadcrumbs for another recipe). Arrange on a platter and serve with the pâté and caper berries alongside. However, if you want to smarten up the presentation, make 'quenelles' with the pâté. Take two teaspoons and scoop up a spoonful of pâté with one. Shape into a rough oval by scraping the portion on to each spoon a couple of times. Place on the toast, garnish with a caper berry and a sprig of parsley.

WELSH RAREBIT WITH WHOLEGRAIN MUSTARD AND ENGLISH ALE

Welsh rarebit is a hearty, bolstering, irresistible mixture of molten cheese, mustard and ale – comfort food at its most indulgent. And while it's sometimes unkindly believed that the English were having a dig at the Welsh in their choice of name – Welsh' was believed to indicate something below standard – it is true that the Welsh are long believed to have revered the combination of cheese and toast.

Serves 2

1 medium egg, separated

1 tbsp wholegrain English mustard

1–2 tbsp light English ale

1–2 spring onions, finely sliced

125g mature Cheddar cheese, grated

4 slices walnut bread

salt and freshly ground black pepper

To serve

1 tbsp sunflower oil

1 tsp white wine vinegar

1 small shallot, finely sliced

a few sprigs of watercress

Preheat the grill to medium. Beat the egg yolk, mustard and ale together in a bowl. Stir in the spring onions, cheese and some seasoning. Then, stir in enough egg white to make a creamy mixture – you may not need all of it.

Lightly toast the bread on both sides. Divide the cheese mixture evenly among the toasted slices and grill until golden.

Whisk together the oil and vinegar, then stir in the shallot and some seasoning. Add the watercress and toss everything together to coat. Serve with the toast.

Much controversy surrounds the origins of this dish's name (it's also known as Welsh 'rabbit'), however, contrary to popular belief, there's very little of the Welsh, or indeed the floppy-eared creature about it.

MUSHROOM FILO TARTLETS

These pretty baskets of filo pastry look stylish yet they're actually extremely easy to make. Fill them with wild mushrooms cooked in this rich, creamy sauce or use your own favourite ingredients.

Makes 6

3 sheets filo pastry
50g butter, melted
1 shallot, finely sliced
350g mixed mushrooms, large ones chopped
3–4 tbsp crème fraîche
1 tbsp chopped chives
salt and freshly ground black pepper

Preheat the oven to 200°C/gas 6. Lightly grease six holes of a muffin tin.

Cut each piece of filo pastry in half, then cut each piece into four squares. Push a square piece of pastry into each buttered hole, brushing well with the melted butter, then continue to layer until each hole has four squares of layered pastry. Bake in the oven for 5–7 minutes, until golden.

Pour the remaining butter into a pan and fry the shallot for 2–3 minutes until softened. Stir in the mushrooms and continue to cook until golden. Remove from the heat and stir in the crème fraîche and half the chives. Season well.

Take the filo shells out of the tin and spoon in the mushroom mixture. Sprinkle over the remaining chives and serve.

A FEAST FIT FOR A KING

Diners sitting down to a meal at a Georgian royal table could expect an elaborate affair; yet before they could take their seats, guests had to grapple with the extensive conventions of contemporary protocol.

The Georgian era marked the height of table etiquette and there were rules governing every aspect of a meal, from how to enter the room – there was a strict hierarchy and order – to when to lift your cup and how to offer food to your neighbour. The table heaved: hosts displayed their wealth by serving several courses, each offering a vast display of dishes and each richer than the last. It's no wonder that the first of the Hanoverian monarchs were such a corpulent bunch. Yet unlike his father and grandfather, King George III adopted a very frugal approach to dining.

Afraid of falling victim to the obesity displayed by his relations, George is renowned for his parsimonious eating habits. He ate sparingly, adopting a predominately vegetarian diet, and is known for breakfasting on boiled eggs – a partiality that was famously mocked by a popular cartoonist of the era. And while previous monarchs may have been regaling their guests with partridge, truffles and elaborate desserts, Prime Minister Henry Addington is said to have complained that when dining with the King, he was served mutton chops and pudding.

Taking in plenty of fresh countryside air was as important to George as his diet, and it was at Kew Palace that he was able to take long walks and nurture this desire for a simple life, away from the stresses of public affairs. The walks were a pleasure he shared with his family, who are known for their love of picnicking together. Servants at the Royal Kitchens at Kew were often called upon to prepare the outdoor repast.

At Kew George was also able to indulge another of his other outdoor passions: a keen interest in agriculture. 'Farmer George' as he was dubbed, was responsible for bringing new and prosperous farming methods to Britain, importing the first flock of merino sheep, which he raised at Kew with a view to improving the national stock.

The gardens at Kew still make a lovely spot for a picnic; so why not take up a time-honoured British tradition and prepare your own finger sandwiches and a jug of homemade lemonade or iced tea.

SMOKED SALMON AND DILL TARTLETS

Light enough not to fill your guests up ahead of all the cakes to follow, yet indulgent enough to be considered a treat, savoury tartlets are a lovely way to start an afternoon tea. In this recipe, ribbons of smoked salmon sit inside a creamy savoury custard, making these pretty as a picture. What's more, they're easy to prepare ahead of your guests' arrival.

Serves 6

200g ready-made shortcrust pastry

a little plain flour, for rolling out

175ml double cream

2 medium eggs, beaten

3 tbsp chopped dill

100g smoked salmon

salt and freshly ground black pepper

Preheat the oven to 190°C/gas 5 and put a baking sheet in to heat.

Roll out the pastry on a lightly floured board until it measures 2–3mm thick and use to line six 10cm individual loose-bottomed tart tins. Chill for 15 minutes. Prick the bases then line each with a piece of slightly crumpled greaseproof paper and fill with baking beans. Bake in the oven on the preheated baking sheet for 15 minutes until the pastry feels dry to the touch and is still pale.

Take the tarts out of the oven and reduce the oven temperature to 180°C/gas 4.

Beat the cream, egg and seasoning together, then stir in the dill. Divide the mixture evenly among the tart tins then arrange strips of smoked salmon on top. Bake in the oven for 20 minutes until the filling is set and very slightly golden on top.

WALNUT SHORTBREADS WITH CREAM CHEESE AND OVEN-DRIED TOMATOES

While these crisp little biscuits could happily be served plain as a lovely savoury bite to accompany a pre-dinner drink, here they've been crowned with a smidgen of cream cheese and tomatoes that have been roasted slowly to intensify their flavour and sweetness.

Serves 6

30g butter, chilled and diced, plus a little extra to grease

65g plain flour

15g walnuts, roughly chopped

a good pinch of salt

1 large egg yolk

For the oven-dried tomatoes

12 cherry tomatoes, halved

olive oil

leaves from a few sprigs of thyme

salt and freshly ground black pepper

To serve

3–4 tbsp cream cheese

thyme sprigs

Preheat the oven to 150°C/gas 2. Start by preparing the tomatoes. Lightly oil a baking sheet and put the tomatoes on top. Drizzle with olive oil then season and scatter over the thyme leaves. Roast for 50 minutes.

For the shortbread, whiz the butter, flour, walnuts and salt together in a small food processor. Tip into a bowl and stir in the egg yolk. Bring together with your hands to make a smooth dough then wrap in baking parchment and chill for 1 hour.

Once the tomatoes are ready, increase the oven temperature to 190°C/gas 5. Roll the dough out on the parchment paper until about 3mm thick. Stamp out 12 rounds using a 5cm cutter, re-rolling the dough as necessary.

Transfer the rounds to a lightly greased baking sheet. Bake in the oven for 12–15 minutes, then cool on a wire rack.

To serve, spread each biscuit with a little cream cheese and top with a tomato half and a sprig of thyme. Store the biscuits in an airtight tin for up to three days.

PARMESAN AND SUN-DRIED TOMATO SCONES

Serving these moreish little savoury scones alongside their sweet counterparts are the perfect balance to all the sugar. They're best served warm straight from the oven with a slick of butter or leave them to cool then halve and fill them with sprigs of pea shoots or watercress.

Makes 8

225g self-raising flour

a good pinch of salt

50g unsalted butter, cubed, plus extra to serve

40g Parmesan, finely grated

3–4 sprigs of thyme, leaves picked

40g sun-dried tomatoes, finely chopped, plus 8 pieces to decorate

125–150ml milk, plus extra for brushing

pea shoots or watercress, to serve

Preheat the oven to 220°C/gas 7. Line a baking sheet with baking parchment.

Sift the flour and salt into a large bowl. Rub the butter into the flour until the mixture resembles breadcrumbs. Stir in the Parmesan, thyme leaves and chopped sun-dried tomatoes.

Make a well in the centre and pour in the milk. Use a round-bladed knife to stir everything together to make a rough dough. Bring it together with your hands then tip it gently on to a board and knead it lightly and quickly until the dough is smooth.

Pat down and shape into a round, about 2.5cm thick. Cut out 8 rounds using a 6cm cutter, re-rolling the dough as necessary, then place on the prepared baking sheet. Push a piece of sun-dried tomato into the top of each one. Brush with a little milk and bake in the oven for 15 minutes, until just golden.

Serve spread with a little butter and stuffed with a few pea shoots or watercress leaves. Store, unfilled, in an airtight container for up to three days.

PRESERVES
AND
DRINKS

SUMMER BERRY CURD

A curd is an unctuous spread made from fruit, butter and eggs – lemon curd being the most traditional and popular (see page 61 for a recipe). Rich, sweet and so wonderfully versatile, a pot of curd is a very useful ingredient to have in your fridge as it can be used to create all manner of desserts. Curds can't be kept as long as jams, but really – they're never around for long enough for anybody to worry about that.

Makes 400ml jar

200g mixed summer berries (raspberries, strawberries, blueberries)

3 medium eggs, beaten

100g unsalted butter, diced

100g golden caster sugar

juice of ¼ small orange

Put the berries in a small food processor and whiz to make a purée. Spoon into a large heatproof bowl. Add the eggs, butter, sugar and orange juice. Rest the bowl over a pan of simmering water, making sure the base of the bowl doesn't touch the water. Stir all the ingredients together with a wooden spoon. Continue to stir the mixture for around 15–20 minutes until it has thickened and coats the back of a spoon.

Pour into a hot sterilised jar, then seal with a lid. Once cool, refrigerate and enjoy within four days.

In the Victorian era, when curds first started to appear, they were served on scones at afternoon tea, but could also be found as fillings for cakes and tarts.

WHISKY MARMALADE

Perk up your morning toast on a cold winter's day with this marmalade that's got a lovely warmth thanks to a healthy splash of whisky. Seville oranges are only in season for a very short period in winter, so if you can't get a hold of them use a standard variety.

Makes around 1.8kg

750g Seville oranges

1.5kg golden granulated sugar

3 tbsp whisky

Cut each orange in half and squeeze out the juice, reserving any pips. Use a metal spoon to scrape out the pith and put in a muslin bag along with the pips. Tie up with string then hang this in a preserving pan or a very large, wide pan.

Put the orange halves into the pan along with the juice and 1.75 litres cold water. Bring to a gentle boil then simmer gently for around 1 hour until the peel is soft.

Take the pan off the heat and lift out the halved oranges. Allow to cool then slice the skins by hand depending on how thick you like the shred.

Return the shred to the pan, then stir in the sugar. Place the pan back on the heat again and heat gently to dissolve the sugar. Bring up to the boil then simmer gently for around 15 minutes, removing any scum. Put two or three saucers in the freezer to chill.

To test whether your marmalade is set, take the pan off the heat and put a spoonful on a saucer. Return the saucer to the freezer for 1–2 minutes. Take it out and draw a wooden spoon through the pool. If it wrinkles it's ready. If not, put the pan back on the heat and test again at 3–5 minute intervals. Stir in the whisky, then spoon into hot sterilised jars and seal with lids. Store in a cool place. Once opened store in the fridge.

BANQUETING HOUSE

Amid the gleaming white stucco façades of one of London's most famous streets, stands the grandest surviving banqueting house in England, the last remaining fragment of the legendary Palace of Whitehall.

The term 'banqueting house' is perhaps something of a misnomer as the structure was not in fact designed for feasting but as an elaborate setting for a new form of court entertainment – the masque. James I replaced Elizabeth I's temporary structure at Whitehall with a grand hall for entertaining.

The divisive Stuart monarch snubbed conventional Jacobean form and created an opulent edifice inspired by refined Italian Renaissance architecture, which was entirely at odds with the restrained Tudor style of its surroundings. It was a controversial construction and one which was to divide opinion for a century, marking a landmark turning point in England's architectural history.

On 30th January each year Banqueting House commemorates one of the most significant events in monarchial history. On a bitterly cold winter's day in 1649, Charles I stepped out of a Banqueting House window on to the temporary scaffold where he was to lose his head. After seven years of fierce fighting, Charles had lost the Civil War to the Puritan Republicans. He was put on trial and found guilty of high treason, a crime for which execution was the only sentence deemed fitting. It is somewhat cruelly ironic that one of the last things Charles was to see as he was walked to his death were the stunning artworks he had commissioned for Banqueting House just a few years earlier. Painted by the famous Flemish artist Rubens, one of the most sought-after painters of his day, the vast baroque canvasses cover the ceiling of its grand hall. They remain one of the most impressive and largest ceiling works from a golden era of art.

In 1698, tragedy struck Whitehall Palace when fire razed all but the Banqueting House and a couple of the palace gates to the ground. The palace was never rebuilt and over the course of the following centuries, Banqueting House was to adopt a variety of roles, from furniture store to royal chapel and concert hall before Queen Victoria offered it up to her people as a museum.

CLASSIC LEMONADE

A chilled jug of homemade lemonade is a wonderful summer drink, the perfect accompaniment to a garden picnic on a warm day. Serve with a sprig of mint to balance the sweetness.

Makes around 400ml cordial

225g golden caster sugar

grated zest and juice of 5 lemons

To serve

mint sprigs

ice cubes

sparkling water

Put the sugar into a pan and add 200ml water. Place the pan over a gentle heat to dissolve the sugar then bring to the boil and simmer for 4–5 minutes until the liquid has reduced slightly and is syrupy.

Add the lemon zest and juice and bring to the boil again. Simmer for 1–2 minutes, then pour into a sterilised jar or bottle and seal.

To serve, put a sprig of mint and a couple of ice cubes into each glass. Add 25ml cordial to each glass and top up with sparkling water.

Sugar was vital to please the royal Tudor palate. Imported from Persia as syrup, it was refined into solid cones called sugar loaves and ground up by the chefs to the required fineness.

ICED TEA

This refreshing and fragrant tea is scented with fennel, ginger and lemongrass. Serve over ice with slices of lemon and for a touch of elegance, chunks of stoned fruit – white peach works well.

Serves 4

1 good-quality English breakfast tea bag

1 tbsp fennel seeds

5cm piece fresh root ginger, finely sliced

2 lemongrass stalks, sliced

To serve

ice cubes

1 lemon, sliced

1 peach, sliced

honey

Put the tea bag, fennel seeds, ginger and lemongrass in a heatproof jug and pour over 1 litre boiling water. Allow to brew for 1–2 minutes then remove the tea bag. Allow to cool.

To serve, put a couple of cubes of ice into a glass, followed by a couple of slices of lemon and peach. Strain 250ml tea into each glass and sweeten to taste with honey.

DAMSON AND GIN JAM

Damsons are a notoriously sour English fruit and not suitable for eating raw but they are perfect for puddings and jams where cooking them in sugar brings out a wonderful deep fruit flavour that is similar to plums. Adding a splash of gin ups the luxury in this delicious preserve.

Makes five 200ml jars
700g damsons
1kg golden granulated sugar
2 tbsp gin

Wash the damsons, picking and discarding any stalks as you go. Put into a preserving pan or very large wide pan with 300ml cold water and bring to the boil. Simmer for 20–30 minutes until the fruit has softened to a pulp and it's coming away from the stone. Give the mixture a good stir – this helps to release the stones from the fruit – then pour in the sugar. Keep the pan over a low heat to allow the sugar to dissolve gradually. Put a couple of saucers in the freezer to chill quickly.

Take a slotted spoon and skim the surface to remove as many stones as you can. Continue to do this, stirring every now and then, which helps them to come to the surface, until you've removed as many as possible.

Increase the heat slightly to bring gently to the boil and cook for around 5–10 minutes. Take the pan off the heat and put a spoonful of jam on to a saucer. Return to the freezer for a minute. Run your finger through the middle of the jam – if it wrinkles, it's ready. If the mixture is still runny, continue to boil and test every couple of minutes. Stir in the gin, then pour into hot sterilised jars and seal with lids. Once opened store in the fridge.

REBELS AND REVELRY

James I was just 13 months old when he was crowned King of Scotland (as James VI). He endured a strict upbringing and deeply religious education under four regents, so it is perhaps no surprise that James was a shrewd, devout and cautious intellectual.

Yet the monarch's demure exterior belied a more rebellious side. When he inherited the English throne in 1603, James was to succumb to the charms of its riches. After the relative poverty of the Scottish regal resources, he was impressed by the luxuries available to him at the English court and began to indulge his newfound wealth.

The royals are renowned for their love of diversion and James I embraced this tradition with gusto. He became a champion of the 'masque', a new and unique form of courtly entertainment. Masques were inspired by the intricate pageants of southern Europe in the late Middle Ages and were mysterious and magical occasions. Poetry, dance, music and song were combined in an elaborate theatrical performance and often courtiers and even the King himself would join in the revelry. Such was the significance of the masque in court life that James I constructed a building at Whitehall Palace specifically for its enjoyment. The great hall at Banqueting House, designed to evoke the grandeur of ancient Rome, was a sumptuous setting for the festivities.

Yet when the wayward monarch built Banqueting House, he also ensured there was a second space for entertaining at Whitehall Palace – a vaulted undercroft beneath the great hall, known as his 'drinking den'. The undercroft was the place where James and his courtiers could retire after the more restrained part of their evening. There they would enjoy riotous drinking sessions and debauched revelry – indeed, it was said that even the ladies abandoned sobriety in pursuit of the pleasures of the vine. Today, Banqueting House continues this festive tradition and the Undercroft, as well as the main hall, can be hired as an imaginative venue for parties.

CHAMPAGNE COCKTAIL

Kick off your afternoon tea in style with this classic champagne cocktail.
It may not be the most traditional of customs but will definitely add a
touch of luxury to the occasion.

Serves 6

6 sugar cubes

6 tsp brandy

Angostura bitters
(optional)

1 bottle champagne or
sparkling wine, chilled

3 strawberries, halved

Put a sugar cube into each glass then pour the brandy
on top and a couple of drops of Angostura bitters,
if using. Top up with the champagne then finish with
a strawberry half.

While the royals may not have
been serving cocktails at their
afternoon tea, they certainly
wouldn't have shied from serving
a tipple alongisde their edible
treats. When travelling, Queen
Victoria and her ladies-in-waiting
are known to have enjoyed
hampers of delicious food served
with 'bottles of hot tea, cream
claret, sherry, seltzer water and
champagne'.

HISTORIC ROYAL PALACES

Five palaces that span nearly a thousand years of history, with a myriad of treasures to share... Historic Royal Palaces is the independent charity that has in its charge five remarkable institutions: The Tower of London, Hampton Court Palace, Kensington Palace, Kew Palace and the Banqueting House. Each of the palaces in our care has survived for hundreds of years.

They have witnessed peace and prosperity and splendid periods of building and expansion but they also share stories of more turbulent times, of war and domestic strife, politics and revolution. These are places where history was made, by kings and queens, politicians and servants, rogues and rebels, craftsmen and traders, philosophers and philanderers, guards and gardeners. The palaces have witnessed strategy, intrigue, ambition, romance, devotion and disaster. World-changing events and the minutiae of everyday domestic life. The grand sweep, and the private moments.

Each palace is symbolic of Britain, and all have world significance. Once they were only for the privileged, now everyone can visit. We give these palaces continuing life. We welcome people, we stage events, we entertain. Our Cause is to explore the stories of how monarchs and people shaped society, in some of the greatest palaces ever built. We warmly invite you to come and enjoy these fabulous buildings; to share their stories and to support us in our work, so that we can give the palaces a future as valuable as their past.

We offer an exciting programme of events and exhibitions throughout the year. Details on this, how to buy tickets and further information about visiting all the palaces can be found on our website. For more information please visit **www.hrp.org.uk** to discover our exciting programme of events and exhibitions throughout the year, plus how to buy tickets and full details of how to plan and enjoy your visit in full.

Visit our online store for our full range of beautiful gifts, including the turquoise and gold fine bone 'Royal Palace' china featured in this book, all inspired by centuries of stories from five amazing palaces.

TOWER OF LONDON

Gaze up at the massive White Tower, tiptoe through a king's medieval bedchamber and marvel at the Crown Jewels. Meet the Yeoman Warders with bloody tales to tell; stand where famous heads rolled and prisoners wept – then discover even more surprising stories about the Tower.

HAMPTON COURT PALACE

Explore Henry VIII's magnificent palace, then stroll through the elegant baroque apartments and glorious formal gardens of William III and Mary II. Feel the heat of the vast Tudor Kitchens and the eerie chill of the Haunted Gallery, before you disappear into the Maze, where whispers of the past will haunt every step to the centre of this topiary puzzle.

BANQUETING HOUSE

Walk in the footsteps of a dazzling company of courtiers who once danced, drank and partied beneath the magnificent Rubens-painted ceiling. This revolutionary building was created for court entertainments, but is probably most famous for the execution of Charles I in 1649. Spare him a thought as you gaze up at this ravishing painting – one of his last sights on earth...

KEW
PALACE

Step inside this tiny doll's house of a palace and sense
the joys and sorrows of past royal lives in intimate detail,
as King George III and his family come to life through a radio
play and display of fascinating personal artefacts. Experience
a riot of colour in authentically re-created Georgian rooms,
before wandering through the eerie rooms of the upper floor,
left untouched for centuries.

Stroll to Queen Charlotte's cottage, built in 1770, where the
royal family enjoyed picnincs and peace in a tranquil corner
of Kew Gardens. Don't miss the tours of the atmospheric
Royal Kitchens – an experience to savour. Re-opened in 2012
and presented 'as found', this rare Georgian survival will spark
your imagination as you sense the presence of the people
who prepared, cooked and served food for the royal household,
almost 200 years ago.

KENSINGTON
PALACE

Take the journey of a courtier through the splendid King's
Apartments and marvel at the impressive rooms and the wall
and ceiling paintings. Or discover the private and personal secrets
revealed with the Queen's State Apartments. Tempted by some
more recent glamour? You'll love the stylish displays celebrating
modern royals, including Princess Diana. Or explore the life,
loves, triumphs and tragedies of Queen Victoria, from lonely
princess to her final years, before enjoying a delicious cream
tea in the elegant Orangery.

INDEX

Historic Royal Palaces is an independent charity. We raise all our own funds and depend on the support of our visitors, members, donors, sponsors and volunteers. The proceeds from the sale of *Tea Fit For A Queen*, as do all our gifts and merchandise, go to support our work, so thank you for buying this book and helping to maintain the beautiful historic buildings for future generations to enjoy.

We would like to thank Nicola Crossley, Alison Pearce and Carey Smith at Ebury and the creative team who produced the book: Jan Baldwin, Imogen Fortes, Emma Marsden, Chris Turnbull, Angela Osgerby, Tabitha Hawkins and Laura Nickoll, as well as Alareen Farrell and Sarah Kilby at Historic Royal Palaces.